Frost Warning

Frost Warning

Poems

Kristine Williams

Sheila-Na-Gig Editions

Frost Warning Copyright © 2026 Kristine Williams
Cover & author photo: Carolyn Highland

ISBN: 978-1-962405-56-0
Library of Congress Control Number: 2026934389

Sheila-Na-Gig Editions
Russell, KY
Hayley Mitchell Haugen, Editor
www.sheilanagigblog.com

Acknowledgments

Women Speak: "After the Memorial Service for My Mother,"
    "Before Dawn, Gura Road," "Falling," "Hollow," "Night
    Music"

Save Lake Logan Association: "Sometimes in Late October"

Native Fruit: "Bombs for Pawpaws"

Advance Praise

As Maya Angelou wisely said, "Easy reading is damn hard writing"—apt words when considering Kristine Williams' powerful and accessible first full-length book of poems, *Frost Warning*. In this collection of universal grievances that enhances both the narrator's and readers' understanding of limitations and possibilities, Williams pulls you into metaphors you have no idea you are entering, metaphors found right there in the stuff of life: glitter after a wedding, cords tangled on a chair. The devil is in the details, after all, and let's face it: that's where we find meaning. The precision of her language, again in the details ("a life clearly bifurcated, / like lightening-struck trees, / alive still, / but twisted / with the effort / of growing around the wound"), speaks to Williams' powers of observation and awareness of what those details symbolize. Once you read *Frost Warning,* you, too, will arrive at a new understanding of what the particulars of your life reveal.

—Deni Naffziger, author of *Strange Bodies*
(Shadelandhouse Modern Press)

For my mother,
Joyce Elaine Stoppenhagen
11/20/38 – 8/31/22

Contents

I.

II.

III.

I.

Sometimes in Later October

after you have cleaned the rental lodge
in the Hocking Hills,
you and your friend walk
the half mile to Lake Logan,
on those few,
perfect
fall days
when wind blows
yellow and orange leaves
in a cyclone around you
and all you want to do
is close your eyes,
listen to the rustle,
smell the dusty,
almost nutmeg-y scent
of a pile of leaves
raked just so,
and it is warm enough
that you've stripped off
your late mother's favorite flannel shirt,
the one you took from the closet
the morning after she died,
refused to wash for months,
until even when you breathed
as deeply as she could not at the end,
nothing of her remained,
and even though watching
lotus invade
and choke Lake Logan of oxygen
makes you remember
how your mother said
it hurt to breathe,
cursed your father
for putting the oxygen mask back on her,
you walk up the hill,

past your favorite small cabin,
the one with the tilted dock,
soaking in the conversation
and the way light reflects
from the water's surface,
those tiny ripples
from a boat
that passed a half mile away,
ripples throwing sparks of light
into the blameless blue sky.
You wish your mother
had given up bourbon,
eaten even when she didn't want to,
had not said *horse shit* when told about
respiratory rehab.
Wish that you could have reached in
and torn out the lungs that did not work,
given her new ones,
made her breathe.

After the Memorial Service for My Mother

I am trying
to find my footing
on what should not be
a slope
or even a gentle incline
but feels like
riding the leading edge
of an avalanche—
tree tops suddenly underfoot,
horizon shifted,
drowning in white.

Mornings the hardest
light pouring in—
all the cracks
in stark relief.

On a Tuesday in Late March

you think about a first line
of a poem that wants to be written
but is caught in the dark threads
of how you miss your mom
and, recently, your dog—
a dog you didn't want at first
but one who was a
constant companion,
who, if she had been a child,
would have been able to drive,
the center of all that you did,
and you think of holes
and empty places,
haunted places,
middle of the night places
where shouting
only makes echoes
that whisper
until they are meaningless.

Last Night

I drive the curves of East Scatter Ridge
with a box of dirty towels from a house I clean,
the grey ones, heavy, over-balancing the washing machine,
the ones I try to hide so guests don't use
every single one,
so I don't have to take them home to wash and dry them,
dirty towels next to a clear plastic box of my mother's sweaters,
one a brown cashmere she would lend me
on weekends home from college,
a box my father loaded because they have to go somewhere,
a box that smells like her,
a box I can't bear to bring into the house yet
because she has only been gone a few months,
and maybe it is a season change
or my birthday coming up
or the Mother's Day gift reminders
I get daily in my email,
but both the towels
and the sweaters
make me angry,
drown out the suddenness of redbuds
and dogwood crowding the hills,
make me weary
in a way I haven't been
since I worked full-time
and was a full-time mom,
when at bedtime for my children
I would discover that I still had more to do,
more obligations,
and now in the back
of the car that used to be my mother's
and that also,
come to think of it,
smells like her,

I carry
two boxes,
two obligations,
one from the past
and one for the future,
neither of which I chose.

Bad Dog

Just when you find the freedom
of longer walks again,
now that your old dog is gone,
just when you hit your stride
in the middle of mile one,
running again now—
breath easing,
the sound of your shoes hitting pavement,
the feel of rolling heel to toe
in the silly-looking Hokas,
a dog surprises you,
comes out of nowhere,
although maybe you were into your podcast,
the one your daughter introduced you to
in the car when you moved her
from Athens, Ohio,
to Richmond, Virginia,
a podcast about serial killers,
and maybe it was your lack of attention,
that you had let your guard down
on this perfect spring morning—
sky cloudless,
breeze cooling the sweat
on your face,
the perfect temperature for a run.

Two bites, over so quickly
you're certain only of pain,
but the niceness bred into women,
of believing that your neighbors,
and even more so, their dogs,
are safe,
evaporates in a moment
when you see blood running
down the back of your leg,

not at all afraid,
not at all like you thought you would feel,
always a little afraid of dogs.

Dog gone somewhere,
you limp home,
at least three cars passing,
none even slowing,
though they had to have seen the blood
and with each hot breath of their passing,
your faith
in kindness,
in people,
leaches away,
replaced now, after, by fear
and tears
as soon as you realize
this means a trip to Urgent Care
and,
silly as it will seem later,
the end of the best run you have had in months.

Home now,
leg still bloody,
you consider how suddenly your house feels
like a refuge
and a prison
and hate that you are afraid,
that what is growing inside you
is ugly and tight,
tastes like a mouthful of pennies.
It shames you a little
that you know better than to google
poisons for dogs,
just in case.

Peonies

At the blue house on Mulberry Street,
I am 10 and
mother says that the ants help open the buds—
black on palest pink,
peonies hanging through the fence
from the neighbor's yard,
Brad, who once climbed the giant pine
in the front yard to rescue our kitten,
stuck and crying for most of a day.
He stuffed her inside his shirt
to leave his hands free to climb,
five pounds of pissed off and scared.
By the time he got down,
the blood soaked through the chambray,
Tell Ginger to use cold water on that,
mother said,
after *thank you,* of course.
She was polite, if a little distant.
They were neighbors but not friends.

That summer,
mother's knife slipped
and when she peeked under the kitchen towel,
slowly blooming red,
she hissed and said swears I had never heard,
told me to run and get Brad because
our one car was with my dad at work.
Hours later she trudged the mile home
from the ER in Lancaster, Ohio,
shoulders defeated.

At dinner, dad puts a vase of peonies on the table in apology,
an apology that ends with black ants all over the uneaten food.
My mother cleans up,
stitched hand wrapped in white gauze,
cries in the kitchen for the second time that day.

Do I Call This Insomnia

I know that it takes
the average person
twenty minutes to fall asleep
but I have been flipping over
and over
and over
for almost an hour now,
know that I should get up,
that the bed is for two things:
sleep and making love,
that neither of those
should become a struggle
associated with my bed,
but hot flashes mostly over
I am frustrated with sleep,
falling asleep too slowly,
awake far too early,
despite knowing the science,
following every recommendation
for better sleep—
a bedtime routine,
a cool, dark room,
eliminating alcohol and screen time
close to bedtime,
getting morning and sunset light
to set my circadian rhythm,
exercising in the right amount
at the right time,
but I have recently come to know
sleeplessness like a lover,
so familiar,
that 5 am waking,
staring at the ceiling,
that *it is going to be a long freaking day*
feeling of defeat,

my husband coming to bed
most nights close to my too early waking,
rolling into the heat and
divot in the mattress topper
sometimes lulling me back
to a dream where I live
a lifetime in those two
extra hours of sleep.
Today, I quit,
dress quietly in the dark
in clothes I shed on the floor,
chilled at this early hour,
but I am still hoping I might sleep,
and with nothing to do today,
I can go back to the bed
and my husband's breathing,
sleep until late morning,
so I don't make coffee,
peach rooibos instead
warm in my hands.
I open the door,
cold hitting me,
the light of dawn
still so far away.

Signs

My friend speaks of tarot cards,
of water and the number 9,
her crystals bounce around the bottom of my purse
in a velvet bag.
I notice feathers daily,
but forget what they represent.

My father tells me he woke from a nap
and saw my mother,
dead for nearly a year,
standing in white shorts
and a red shirt,
that the cat sometimes sits up
as she often did before my mom
walked into a room,
that he misses just talking with her,
admits that he still sometimes does.

Signs and portents
and runes in the clouds,
a cardinal tattooed inside my forearm.
Reminders of my mother
everywhere,
but nothing can replace her,
her voice in old messages still on my phone,
always beginning the same way:
Hi. It's your mom.

Night Music

You remember that he broke you,
that rich boy,
in it for the novelty of slumming
with the used-to-be-fat girl
who had lost inches,
learned how to say *fuck you*
with confidence she almost felt,
so you ran home,
but you don't know why
what you remember so clearly
about the friend who took you in
is driving at night,
riding with her through Atlanta
at 3 a.m. in her silver Corvette,
the band, Yes, and complex guitar licks,
fog and bugs
forming haloes around
arc sodium lights,
impossibly tall over the empty highway.
Why were you in a car
in the middle of the night
with the friend who let you stay
in her apartment for days
after that boy dumped you?
You slept through the day with her
after she nursed NICU babies all night.
When you dragged yourself back to OU,
back to grad school,
broken bits loosely knitted,
you looked your advisor in the eyes,
the one who once said:
it sounds like you're bringing me a problem, with disdain,
said someone died unexpectedly
to cover your absence.

Lying came easily after that,
sometimes even when it wasn't necessary,
one lie building on the last,
sometimes hard to keep them straight.
The ease of it after a while,
lying because you could,
especially to yourself.

Lines

Draw a single line,
thick on white canvas.
It can be slightly askew,
can be the horizon.
Or a crack
where darkness seeps in.
Draw the line with confidence.
Remake your definition of *level*.

Do people wait *in* line? Or *on* line?
Think about lines at the airport,
snaking around poles and ribbons.
Do you imagine jumping over?
Make that ducking under.
The wheels of your carry-on rattling
and rolling, spinning
against the cracks in the tile,
white floor stretching out
for what seems miles,
wheels whispering about waiting
and wondering when things will begin.

Faceless people waiting,
maybe waiting to see a horizon,
a red sun disappearing into the sea,
all around them right now
black and white and gray,
the color of waiting and of lines.

Waiting

The waiting room
at Fairfield Medical Center is empty—
even the woman at the desk
has come to explain how to contact a nurse if I have
questions,
says she *has* to go home
and I almost say
get to, you mean
but bite my tongue
because she has kind eyes
and I am tired and afraid
if I open my mouth I will cry
because I am waiting
in the same place
we waited for my mom's surgeon
a year ago
when the kidney was so infected
she got sepsis
and it was the beginning of the end
which is why I am here
with my dad,
his person now,
as they implant a pacemaker
that will keep his heart rate regular
and his heart,
broken and barely begun to heal,
pumping blood regularly,
my mom gone like falling asleep:
sinking slowly,
then darkness
all at once.

Summer, 1976

It was July
in the house on Mulberry Street,
Lancaster, Ohio,
the faded blue one
with the sagging porch,
the one with the peonies
crawling with ants,
where your parents brought
a beagle puppy
who got sick and
your mother blamed you
because you liked to touch
her cold, wet nose
and she said
you should have left her alone.
The house where fights were hushed
because the neighbors were so close,
separated only by a chain-link fence
and some spindly roses,
the house where you watched
mother sprinkle water on handkerchiefs
with an old Coke bottle
topped with a plastic rose with holes
before we could afford a steam iron,
make cotton smooth and crisp
on the board
set up in the family room,
steam rising and hissing
over the sound of Dark Shadows
and trucks rumbling past
to bring beer to the
Avondale Market up the street,
the one where you took old bottles,
bought Jolly Ranchers,
always cherry,

with the deposit,
mouth sore,
tongue bright red,
in your room on the second floor,
where that puppy,
hand-fed and nursed back to health
by a local vet,
was not allowed,
howling sometimes from the doghouse
in the backyard,
against the alley,
wanting to come in
as badly as you dreamed of escape.

After the Wedding

I drive three hours to a wedding
I don't really want to attend,
but my daughter has asked,
so I buy a used dress,
pack a toothbrush,
and drive 3 hours through misty rain
listening to a podcast I barely hear,
the map on display counting down
miles left in the trip as
trucks spray water from tires
even after the rain stops,
leaves mostly gone
in southwest Ohio,
but what remain are
a red so dark
it looks like dried blood
under low, dark clouds.

One of my daughter's friends,
one of the last to marry,
has chosen an outdoor venue
at the end of October
so I shiver in a mostly sleeveless dress,
a red that clashes with the soft green
of my daughter's bridesmaid dress,
a dress that cost over $400 to have altered,
a dress she later strips off,
hands to another bridesmaid,
says *throw it away.*
I need room in my suitcase.
I gather it up and say I will take it,
have it cleaned
and she laughs,
says this is the fourth wedding
in a year,

four dresses she will never wear again,
as she strips bobby pins and rosebuds
from her friend's hair,
then her own,
does the messy bun
I always wish I could do
but never can
and when I ask her how she does it,
she says if she thinks about it,
it never works.
Later, I prove how cool I am
by doing shots of a vile,
wormwood-based liquor from Chicago
in our hotel room,
laugh until the drama turns ugly
and there are tears,
but I know this is how a drunken party ends,
so I close the bathroom door,
survey dirty towels,
washcloths stained with makeup
on the floor,
think about the glitter
and trash
left after the wedding,
and I wonder about
young women who think,
like I know my mother did in 1960,
that this one day,
if pulled off without a hitch,
will somehow guarantee happiness,
will offset distances and silences,
call the day perfect
even when it is not,
set up a pattern
they will repeat for years to come.

Cooking Curry in Athens, Ohio

My husband stops at the door
to the dining room,
closes his eyes,
inhales deeply
and says *Amanabad.*
I make Gujarati potatoes
and dahl,
vegetable biryani,
and am just about to drop the
cauliflower, coated in chickpea batter,
into the oil to fry.
I am no match for his mother,
who in 1970
traveled to India with four children
under the age of 10.
In pictures her lipstick is always perfect,
chin raised.
She made curries so spicy
yogurt was a must on the table.

We take the meal the three miles
to the house now falling
slowly into disrepair,
piles of cookies in the living room,
cords tangled on a chair.
Containers without lids
clutter the kitchen counters,
the ones that used to be scrubbed
and spotless.
My father-in-law is still in his pajamas
at 2 in the afternoon.
My mother-in-law,
who often now forgets to wear shoes,
sweeps the deck again and again,
becomes angry if we try to help,

asks the same questions over and over,
dementia such a cruel disease.

Once we remind her
that it is Tuesday,
the day we have been bringing dinner,
my mother-in-law inhales like her son did
as I remove lids,
can't remember the word *cauliflower*,
but can tell me exactly which spice
I left out of the garam masala,
how the pakora are greasy
because the frying oil was not hot enough.

What Would I Give?

When we pick him up at the airport,
I swear my son's shoulders are wider
than when I saw him 6 months ago,
muscles in his biceps strain the fabric of his shirt.
His hair is certainly longer,
though still the color of the copper mugs
the West End Cider House uses for Moscow mules,
collecting your driver's license
so you don't steal one,
and I remember misty fall mornings
when he was in high school,
driving him to the top of the driveway
to wait for the bus to Athens High School,
watching him make his way to the middle,
slouching into a seat.

I think about how time speeds up
as we grow older,
bonds stretched but not fraying,
how I feel it more than my children,
try not to cling,
try not to mark every tiny loss—
moving, marrying, having children—
though that is what I want to do,
know that if I am lucky,
they will continue after I am gone
as I have after my mother's death.

Wish on a star.
Hold your breath past a graveyard.
Now, I have no magic charm
but I would give up anything,
hell, everything,
for that laugh,
open and deep and raucous

from the living room
as I turn into the warmth of the bed
pass into dreaming
without even knowing when
I crossed that edge.

II.

January in Athens County

Days of cold
and snow
and quiet
lead to contemplative thoughts
of your mother,
gone for nearly six months,
of deer
under the hickory tree,
and how
even though the days
grow longer,
it feels darker—
clouds clog the sky,
grey against lighter grey,
snow falls,
the hush
felt in our bones,
how the wind
tightens the flesh
over cheekbones,
thin already,
now burning.

Sunlight slanting in,
a cup of jasmine tea,
hands wrapped around the cup,
the warmth real
and spreading.

Winter Weather Advisory for Athens County

The neighborhood is still,
dogs walked while the sun was still shining,
weak and washed out as it was,
shopping done
before the predicted storm,
busses roaring past
with loads of children
wanting only to get home,
find books and cookies,
maybe freshly baked
by distracted mothers
worried about partners
getting home
safely
before the snow.

The library, empty now,
closing early because of weather,
dark by the river,
white powdery snow
blown into the spaces
only winter can find,
soughing through cracks
in the weatherstrips
around windows,
months to go before
it will be warm again.

I walk on the bike path,
determined to walk as I always do on Tuesdays,
hoping my Subaru can get me home,
as it has so often,
but hurrying still,
not willing to tempt getting stuck
on the hill to our house,

remember how many times
I had to park at the bottom
and walk the half mile home,
slipping on ice,
often in the dark,
almost always alone.

When My Son Was Six

I left him alone
at the fence to a ride
at the Athens County fair.
He was too small to ride
and my daughter begged and begged,
but could not ride alone,
and it was August
and I was tired,
a ride called The Himalayan,
kind of a kiddie rollercoaster
meets merry-go-round
that went forward and backward
in a circle;
my son, wearing a tie-dyed shirt,
flashed by every time we went around
and it was only once we started
and there was no way I could get off,
that it occurred to me
that this was a fair
and there were so many ways
he could get lost or hurt
or taken,
the smell of popcorn
and hay
and the dirt
stirred up by
all those people,
a pregnant teen and her
acne-faced boy
arms around each other's waist,
hands tucked into the other's
back pockets,
tired looking parents
carrying the remnants of
an elephant ear

or cotton candy
or that lemonade with half a lemon
bobbing inside.

My son was fine
and I hugged him fiercely
until he pushed me away.
Of course he was fine,
otherwise this would be
an entirely different poem.

Frisson

you explain,
six feet of lanky, loose-jointed boy
slouched in the passenger seat,
finger stabbing at the console,
that feeling at the end of *this* song,
it shatters my spine.
Do you ever feel like that, Mom?

And I still my tongue
but in my head I make a list:
The first time I saw your long, newborn fingers.
The way your hair curls over your collar
no matter how many times
you wet and comb it.
The time I saw you hold that girl's face,
framing it with your hands,
before you leaned in
and I turned away.

Every day I know you,
is what I wish I'd said.

The Weight of Broken Things

Your side of the bed,
empty for days now,
is easy to make in the morning,
the cat almost as warm
but too small
to keep my feet warm.
I say this,
try to make a joke,
your voice on the phone
our only contact
for more than a week.
Children raised
and scattered to east and west,
we thought we were in the clear,
thought we could stop
being vigilant and worried,
only to find ourselves
where so many of our friends have,
caring for parents
who once cared for us,
and we swear
we will make it easy for our children,
as I doubt our parents
of that generation did,
who thought it was their due
to be cared for,
that they were owed,
and I know how that sounds
even as I say it,
and I try not to fill with resentment,
though after almost no sleep
for days, that tone creeps in
when we discuss
cleaning out the basement,
putting plans on paper

to shield our children
from bearing this burden of care,
even as my father scoffs,
says how overprotective
we always have been
of our children,
how when I went to college
my mother took along an apron,
cut the strings,
with her, not even a joke.
I tell you to take a breath,
count to ten
before you change the dressing
on your father's head
again,
you, miles from home
and sleep
and comfort.

Moving Day

I watch my children
run right over the edge
of what they know,
gather their courage,
pack it
in the same boxes
as their clothes,
stuffed down tight,
tape them closed,
lift, carry, load
into dark,
diesel-smelling trucks,
drive through flat Kansas
and traffic clogged Brooklyn streets,
the destination
only the start.

Driving My Son to the Airport

Although I have made this trip,
driving from Athens to the airport
in Columbus, Ohio,
at least a half dozen times in the last year alone,
it is 3:00 in the morning
with fog so thick
nothings seems real,
much less recognizable.
I have not slept much
and feel groggy
and clumsy
behind the wheel of a car,
my late mother's,
that is still not familiar.

I am taking my son,
who surprised me for Mother's Day
with a visit from Denver
where he has lived for the last two years,
to catch a flight home,
the cheapest he could find,
because he is 28
and unemployed at the moment,
one of those 6 am flights
with two connecting flights
with minutes to spare between,
and what I feel besides
uncoordinated behind the wheel
is guilty that I have not
gone to visit him yet.

Fog swirls around the lights
set far above the bypass

and I feel claustrophobic
and lost in what should be
familiar territory.
My son's voice grounds me:
What's your favorite part of The Bible?
I say *Grace*—
the idea that I cannot earn Heaven
but then I wonder if I really mean
my favorite part of being his mom.

This Summer

My daughter sends pictures from Greece,
hammocks over pools,
views of an ocean
a shade of blue
I have never seen before
except in paintings.
She is with friends
she has known for years,
friends from all over the US,
friends who all turn 30 this year.

I open her pictures
while I am cleaning an Airbnb,
windows open
because the entire house
smells like whatever the guest
cooked for breakfast
and I am sweating because
it is in the 90s today,
has been all week
and will be for days.

I remember summer days
spent at my grandfather's cottage
on Lake James in Indiana,
learning to water ski,
riding across the misty lake
early in the morning
to get donuts at Tom's,
a dozen donut holes
my grandfather and I
secretly shared on the trip back,
pillowy bites of yeasty sweet.
This summer has been
fraught with parent worries,

cleaning houses
but ignoring the gardens
I simply don't have the heart for
since my mother's death,
the heat like a weight.
I text my friend:
I can be packed for California in an hour,
know I will instead
spend that hour
on my knees
scrubbing toilets,
checking for things left behind under beds.

The Meeting

In the deep ditch of January,
the sheets are cold
as I slide in, naked,
pull the cover over my head
until all that is uncovered is my nose.
Later, caught in the web of a dream
half-remembered,
I wake and am lost
for a moment
until I hear soft guitar chords from the living room,
know that soon
you, warm and smelling of beer,
will slide
past the chilled part
of our bed
into the warmth
and impression
I have made
in the memory foam topper,
throw a leg over mine,
your hand gripping my hip,
and that I can stop chasing
a dream of my mother
gone now for months.

Late Night on Gura Road

The alarm chimes
softly at 3:30,
the night still,
cold,
and I am dressing
in the dark,
boots tonight,
you moving beside me
hand warm,
strong,
around mine
and of course you have a flashlight
and shine it
not where you are walking or on the path
but where I need to be—
so typical—
lighting the way
to the top of the hill,
the place where I stopped with the old dog
so she could rest,
and now we are here
at the place where the
neighborhood is laid out
at our feet
looking at the moon,
bright in a cloudless sky—
the last lunar eclipse
for three years,
something my mother will never see.

When we met
I would drive through
Uptown Athens
late at night
because I could always find your motorcycle,

the one with the fairing
you painted blaze orange
after that car pulled out
right in front of us and
you kept us upright,
God knows how,
and on those years ago nights
I would drive by,
know where you were,
not needing you yet,
just the knowledge of you.

Tonight I see that boy
under the
worry so often there now,
your parents,
my widowed dad,
car repairs
and yard work,
but there you are,
the boy I loved so fiercely
holding me
against you
in the dark
under a moon growing dim
as a shadow
spills across,
hiding her face
and yours,
but only briefly.

Falling

My dad talks about falling,
but at this point in our conversation,
I am not sure
if he means falling down in his house
or falling in love
with the woman he met
after my mother died,
him lost and not eating,
wandering through his days
anchored by a stray cat,
taken in by my mother
just before she became ill,
and finding love
across the aisle at church,
with a woman who looks like
my mom from the back,
and honestly, I am not sure
he knows either.

So similar:
falling down
and
falling in love.
Both leave you
on the ground,
looking up at,
say, the underside
of the kitchen counter,
happening in an instant,
you not knowing
what just happened.
Was it an earthquake?
A stroke?
The result is the same—
you on your ass,

legs splayed
in the least dignified way
you can think of,
dazed and
bruised,
maybe bloody,
wondering what day it is,
where you are
in your world.

Or maybe you see it coming,
a love so
treacherous,
a slope
so dangerous,
you would be
a fool
to continue,
and yet you do.
Landing on your feet
this time,
only a little battered,
lucky you did not
break something,
like a rib,
or a heart.

Vernal Equinox

I.

Lift your chin into
slanting sun,

windows in need
of a good spring clean—

vinegar and water,
newspapers balled up—

spray the paper,
not the glass.

II.

Spring is hard,
all that getting out and doing,

when you have not minded
being at home alone most days.

Forget about a friend's post,
and feeling left out.

You never ask to go along on adventures,
hope to be asked,

and suddenly this feels like
high school, you fat and shy,

wanting to fit in,
to be the fun friend people want around,

on a day so fine and fair
your heart breaks twice:

once from the beauty of the sky,
again later, from feeling alone.

Another Frost Warning Tonight

Far into May, we cover tender buds
against the bite of frost, get creative
because there are so many, the iris too tall for sheets,
so I find old socks, stretch them over the iris buds,
so my garden looks like witches crashed,
lost their shoes, left only stocking feet,
spindly legs, sticking up.
I rise early to snatch away the assortment
of old socks: tube socks from my son's
abandoned dresser, the Christmas socks
with silver thread that scratch uncomfortably,
ugly brown and stained and mismatched.

But those iris from the house behind the big church
where I grew up, blue flag and purple and white,
remind of the split-rail fence, the screened porch
where we ate summer meals at a picnic table
moved from the apartment in Chicago,
my parents a young couple, two children, too poor
for something nicer, then consigned to the porch,
macaroni salad swimming in Miracle Whip,
green onions from the garden, stored in a glass of water,
taken out one at a time, jockeying for the biggest,
dipped in salt, bitter bite, gritty crunch.
The rhubarb grew at one end, and there was pie
hot from the oven, my mother's crust
I still can't make reliably, flaking and buttery
on my tongue, the sweet-tart of rhubarb,
sugar caramelized in the bottom,
dinner at exactly 6:00, the menu planned
weeks ahead on the calendar by the sink
where I dried dishes as my mother washed.

I want to go back to that house, marked by iris
in the spring, remake the talk over washing dishes,

tell my mother it would be OK, that her Celiac disease,
lying dormant
like the corms of the iris through the winter,
would make her as creative in her cooking
as my using socks on the tall, fragile stems of my iris,
her gluten intolerance would be more manageable
than the lymphoma it dragged behind,
the treatments she called *chemo* even though it was not,
biological therapy not sounding dramatic enough.

III.

Spring in Athens, Ohio

Daily,
it seems,
I carry the mice
caught in our live traps,
because I can't forget
the broken-back one,
struggling to crawl,
across the yard
and street.
My father says
they will just come back
but my soft-hearted husband
says that if they are smart
and brave enough
to find a way back in,
he finds no problem
with carrying them
as much as a quarter mile away,
releasing them,
sometimes reluctantly clinging
to the slippery plastic of the trap,
into the underbrush,
matted leaves
and winter-spindly trash brush
near the ravine.
Today the air is kind
and smells of spring—
wet concrete, dark earth—
and I tuck the trap
behind the mailbox,
set off for a run
outside for the first time
in months,
stretch muscles
cramped by too much

sitting inside
an all-electric house
that is cold all damn winter,
search through all of the
exercise options on my watch,
reflection of my winter routine:
Pilates, yoga, elliptical,
indoor walk,
indoor run,
hit outdoor run,
and feel the freedom
before I am through
the first mile,
like that mouse,
clinging to the safety
of being inside,
in the known,
but now relearning
the freedom
of being small
in such a big world.

Before Dawn, Gura Road

In the single digits, it is mind-numbingly cold,
not that my mind has caught up to my body,
which dressed in the dark, by touch and the memory
of where I threw clothes on the floor by the bed,
before I got between chilled, white cotton only a few hours ago.
My shirt is on backward I realize,
tag scratching the hollow that sucks in when I breathe,
although I am trying to take shallow breaths
through the collar of my puffy coat
so the hair inside my nose doesn't freeze.
I am ankle-deep in snow
while my dog picks her way through the yard
trying to find the perfect place to pee
and I am trying not to be irritated
because I was, after all, the one who gave in, got up,
snapped on the harness and leash
(coyote yip-yips earlier have made me cautious).
But now that we're here,
I see how the snow glitters where my flashlight touches,
flakes dance, caught in the beam,
and above,
the Milky Way, gauzy,
and suddenly I remember a box of letters I found once:
two women writing to each other through winter and a pandemic
but beneath their words,
reaching out,
connecting,
driftwood from a sinking ship,
something to cling to in the middle of the vast, deep blue
and, buoyed by the memory,
I stop and the universe unfurls above.
Snow hides the ugliness of winter, crunches beneath my boots,
and I stop my breath,
listen to the blood *whooshing* in my ears,
hear also a train whistle,

the dogs down the street barking,
anticipate the warmth of the bed,
knowing you will roll close no matter how cold my skin,
hold me until I fall back to sleep.

Poetry Retreat, Chesterhill, Ohio

I.

I am sweating
on a humid late June morning,
but my bare feet are rooted
in grass gone brittle
by summer heat
and little recent rain
and I am doing Qigong
for the first time,
feeling a tingling
as my hands gather energy,
create a ball,
rotate it
once,
twice,
three times,
imagine that energy reduced
to a bright pearl,
store it in my belly.

Later in the day,
a horse named Popcorn
lets me lean against his neck,
find an itchy spot inside his back leg,
bobs his head,
half closes his eyes
with the simple pleasure of it
and I feel it too,
his heart four times the size of mine
beats slowly,
as I match his ease,

and for a moment,
we just breathe.

II.

Above the hammocks
at the Resting Place
in Adams County, Ohio,
the tops of trees
toss their heads,
caught in a summer wind,
the wind running before a storm
that has loomed all day,
yet the base of the tree
is firm,
rooted,
unmoved by wind
or rain,
moved
only by lightening
like some of the others,
split trunks healing
and growing around wounds.

I have driven the 30 minutes
from my home in Athens, Ohio
for a day of wellness
and horses
but finally admit at lunch
to the other four retreat participants
that I have never been
close to a horse
and that I am frightened
by their big teeth,
their size and
that my husband described them
as basically big, mean dogs.

My horse guide checks with me
every step of the way,

am I comfortable letting
the horses smell
the backs of my hands
held through a gate?
Am I ready to walk into the barn?
Every move of every horse,
explained,
body language
and nonverbal communication,
a subject I loved teaching
for over thirty years
at a two-year college
I now resent enough
to avoid,
deliberately,
naming.
My last years so toxic,
so taxing that the memory alone
exhausts me.

I wash the dust of the barn
and the horse
from my hands in the bathroom,
my eyes underlined
with purple smudges,
too many sleepless nights,
nights filled with loss
and worry about my widowed father,
my own clarity,
a life clearly bifurcated,
like lightening-struck trees,
alive still,
but twisted
with the effort
of growing around the wound.

What Would I Buy?

For Kari

Coming out of a curve
in the foothills of Tennessee
where we have had a poetry weekend,
my friend says that I must write a poem
about the place that just caught my eye,
wondering about what one might find there.

What would I buy at a store
called The Gittin' Place?
Crammed into a strip mall
on a curve in the middle
of miles of two-lane road
where Google Maps has sent us:
a route that promises to cut 30 minutes
from an almost 6 hour trip.

Could I get my mom back there,
gone now for 18 months?
And if so,
what would my father do
with his new lady friend,
and he does stress *friend*,
although my brother and I know better.

I could buy material
leftover from some grandmother's quilt,
tiny roses in pink and red,
or a blue with dots of white,
oddly shaped pieces,
the shape of an armhole
in a checked green cotton.
Would I make a quilt?
A project that has always seemed

like too much commitment,
days or months or years
hunched over a frame or a hoop,
because it must be hand-stitched,
rows of stars
or log cabin squares.

Teeny, careful, even stitches
have always seemed beyond me
but I know it would have made
my mother proud.

Could I sell things at The Gittin' Place?
The extra 10 pounds
that have dogged me for several years.
The junk my husband collects,
crammed into spaces I want to use.
The snow that might fall this week,
well into April.
Who would even want those things?

Bombs for Pawpaws

Last week,
I was angry for days,
because animals beat me
to most of the pawpaws growing
at the edge of the yard.

I am on my knees
at the edge of the yard,
while bombs fall in Israel.

I gather the remaining pawpaws,
each soft as a peach,
to make jam,
while bombs fall in Israel.

I am on my knees.
How dare I complain?

Later,
I walk with my husband,
hand wrapped securely in his,
while across an ocean,
a woman holds the cooling hand
of her child,
killed by rubble from their home,
on her knees,
while bombs fall.

How the size of the world
shrinks
to the size of the tragedies
we survive.

Hero Worship

With my tongue, I set stories singing.
Stories stolen from sighing spruce trees.
                              —*The Kalevala*

In the dream,
she falls,

cries trapped behind frozen lips,
cheeks wet with tears.

She remembers a copper box
and a boy, her hero, offering it,

saying he had plucked stories
from fields of golden wheat and silent water

lays them at her feet,
an offering,

begs to start again
go back to the beginning,

untangle knots of words,
pick apart threads with his teeth,

empty every secret
on the floor in slanting sunshine,

lay the story bare and
open the hurt to light and air:

Surely they have earned this.
She pushes at his boundaries,

digs at wounds she has always known
were there, makes him weak,

forces down
walls that grew for years,

until he is exposed
for the lies he told

until the sky breaks open
and into the thunder she screams

words she held for years
behind the net of her teeth.

After the dream,
she can find no footing

her life, turned upside down,
made unfamiliar overnight,

the box shattered on the ground.

Things That I Try to Forget

The shirt I took
from my father's closet,
smelling faintly of Aqua Velva
and Tide detergent,
when I left for
my freshman year
at Miami University,
a shirt I slept in for years.

When I was 19 and fell in love
with my brother's friend
who left for boot camp
at the end of the summer,
no cell phones or internet,
he called when he could,
talked to my roommate
when I was not there,
waiting in line for a pay phone,
hurried conversations,
then *I have to go so someone else
can use the phone.*

The car I borrowed to drive
to the Cincinnati airport
to pick him up after three months,
a battered silver,
(but rust the most prominent color).

The silence of him
and my not knowing
how to fill it.

The pain
of our breaking.

The absence of him
after talking for months,
the ghosting completely out of the blue.

Shooting Pool on Yet Another Friday

I say
It's too complicated to explain
But in my head I think
If you had been paying attention
I wouldn't have to explain at all,
music too loud,
pool balls break and roll.
I'm off my game tonight
and want to punch
the older guy who keeps saying
You're over-cutting everything tonight
even though I have never punched anyone in my life,
or my husband saying
When's the last time you played?
which is supposed to excuse me somehow
but I want to stand on the pool table
crammed in the back of the Cat's Eye
on Court Street, Athens, Ohio,
tables that are not level,
one bumper drooping
and every drunk in the place
walking by because the tables
are right by the toilets
which are,
thank God,
at least as early as we play on Fridays,
clean and have toilet paper
although some of the graffiti
confuses me,
stand on the table and scream
that my mother is dead
and dead so quickly that
no one even had time to process
and hospice barely arrived
before she was gone,

that it has been
months
since I played,
since I played well,
since I cared about playing,
that I have two states now:
pissed at everyone and everything
or
not giving a shit
which is where I am tonight,
and I wonder how you can shoot pool
game after game
Friday after Friday
and not want to claw your eyes out
from boredom.
I dread the question
wanna shoot some pool?
because
no,
no, I do not want
to spend one more night
being the only woman,
sipping a low carb hard seltzer,
either proving a point about women and pool
or
surprising people with a competent game
and
I know my husband and I will have yet another
what are we eating for dinner
endless discussion
because
did you miss that
I
don't
care?
Not about much of anything
and even less about

food
or getting the ball to draw or angles
when the Fridays string out behind us
unchanged
except where we play
the future I can't even consider
stretches out ahead
in an unbroken line.

Restorative Yoga at the Pilates Studio

I am lying on a thick mat
with my feet on the cold, wooden floor
of the Pilates studio.
The sound of singing bowls
are supposed to make me relax
deeply,
but only distract,
with the irregular rhythm
and two are dissonant
and my tinnitus is a completely
different pitch
and now that I am partially relaxed,
a muscle under my shoulder blade
has started its own singing
and it hurts
and I try not to squirm,
to *let go,*
but all I can think is that this is so much noise,
and then a gong
that I feel in my chest
and molars
and like flipping a switch,
my muscles relax,
I see colors swirl in the dark
and the grief,
the grief that I say is OK,
that is not intrusive
but really is
and present every single damn day,
floods my throat
and I choke back tears
and Karena touches my forehead,
whispers not-words
and I let the tears run
and pool under my head,
the release
I thought I would never find
finds me.

The Kiss

In 1979, I was the nice, fat girl,
a good student, dependable babysitter,
the one who followed the rules,
lettered in Forensics, which,
we had to explain to Coach Miller,
meant "debate team, sort of."

My first kiss was in the back of a station wagon,
two weeks shy of turning 16,
another couple on the front bench seat,
parked in the dark at St. Bernadette's,
with the quarterback of the Lancaster Golden Gales,
God knows why.
He got the real me instead of
the sassy girl of all of those teasing notes
passed in 8th period Geometry
(I always was better on paper)
the ones I stored in the space behind the top of the closet door
in my yellow and white bedroom, the four-post bed
I begged for and my parents couldn't afford but
bought anyway on their first-ever credit card
and that I just expected as my teen due.
He said beautiful girls never thought they were
and I didn't know if he was being kind
or even talking about me.

Later that year his prom date told me he said that
kissing me was like kissing his sister and, when he heard,
he casually dragged my chair, 5th period lunch,
into the middle of the room, kissed me in front of everyone,
taking his time, crooked grin,
sauntered back to class, said "sister, my ass,"
which earned him a detention.
Not the kissing, mind you, the language.

Hollow

Anger like that leaves you hollow,
leaves you open
which would be ok any other day
except today you are driving and listening
to 80s on 8 on Sirius XM and
of course the Scorpions are singing
about *still loving you*
and your mind pokes at that 40-year-old memory hole,
like a tongue in a bloody, used-to-be tooth hole
pain exquisite but you just can't help yourself
and here you are feeling the loss of some long ago not-ending
with a boy you have written at least a dozen poems about
and who, damn you, you still long for
in a way that somehow grows sharper with time
and you want to crank the volume and drive,
backroads where redbuds and dogwood rule,
maybe wail,
think about what might have tried to but never could have been.
Instead, you turn right off of County Road 25, onto Gura Road
and up the hill, around the curve,
peepers in the pond singing their own song
and you know tonight they will be so loud
they will drown out everything else.

Bathsheba After Bathing on a Roof

He calls you here,
what choice do you have?
But you think,
so smug,
manage to stop the words
before they escape,
coated with contempt.

You know the power of a woman,
naked,
bent at the waist
to wash an ankle,
hair a wet rope
trailing down a back the color of honey,
as you wash away the dust of this city,
because here he is,
thinking he's a king,
broken and
begging,
undressing you with his eyes,
though he's already seen it all—
a peeping
little
thief.

In the end,
when he has finished with you,
what you are sure he thinks of as his conquest,
ruined your life because he had the power to,
all you feel is emptied by
this man who thought he knew
the mysteries of his God.

No Glass Slippers Appear in Chauncey, Ohio

My friend says
she feels like Cinderella,
the washing up,
the chores,
never at an end.
She helps to raise
her grandson,
takes him to school,
makes meals,
while his parents
work full-time
as they have to
since their divorce
and the pandemic.
Over iced matcha
at our favorite table
at Donkey Coffee,
the one we can only get
in the summer
when the OU students are gone,
we talk about
marriages gone sideways
and of leaving Ohio
for California
or France
or Italy,
sharing pictures
of houses badly
in need of repair
but cheap enough
we could afford them.
I joke that all I need
is a bathing suit,
three pairs of shorts,
half a dozen t-shirts

and one sexy, black dress,
say we can live on
bread and cheese and wine.
When it is bad at home,
I text:
I can be packed in an hour,
knowing I will instead
stew silently
in that way
a child of the 60s,
and a girl,
was taught.
Impotent,
although my friend
says she learned
many years ago
and the hard way,
never, ever to use that word
with her husband
who came as close
to slapping her as he ever has
and all for a word
that perfectly describes
her marriage
everywhere outside
the bedroom.

Making Risotto

It has been 812 days
since your death,
mother, and still,
a thousand reminders
crowd out the blue sky,
crows circling
and crying
in rusty voices,
the humidity of June
in SE Ohio,
iris come and gone,
the battle with deer
over lilies just begun.

All day I have dreamed
of your hands,
mine now so like them,
veined and spotted,
stirring stock,
one ladle at a time,
into risotto,
standing over the
same stove,
same copper pan
you used for everything.

That pan, now mine,
holds onions,
rosemary, and rice
I stir to brown the outside.
Later I will add wine and stock,
stir and stir and stir,
Parmesan at the end,
beaten with a wooden spoon,
your secret to the creamy texture.

In the background,
a riot of color,
sunset, come later

and later until soon,
light outlasts the dark.
The reminders of you
never balancing,
still distracting
from the taste of risotto,
the beauty of this day.

My Life Is Not a Taylor Swift Soundtrack

My daughter's face,
as she surveys the collection
of Taylor Swift CDs in my car,
is a little horrified,
and yes,
I went a little crazy
once I found this music
in my 60s,
so I shrug and ask
What era do you want?
and while I am not sorry
for the CDs,
music that has
pulled me back from the brink
(please don't ask *of what?*
because you know),
what I cannot say to my daughter
is that I am ashamed
in a way I have not been
since I was caught
sneaking back into my house
in the summer of 1981
and making my father cry,
for my reason for loving this music,
the broken-hearted-but-damn-you-you-can't-break-me lyrics
that I have played over and over
and over and over,
memorized, screamed in my car,
all because I was not careful
with my heart. Again.
Thirty-something years into
a marriage, I trusted my husband
to understand a rant
about my father
not acknowledging

the anniversary of my mother's death,
instead texting that he is off to *b'fast*,
with his new girlfriend,
the one who taught him
things like *b'fast*,
and about emojis,
and instead of the support
I assumed my partner
would offer,
or even not saying a word,
or his usual *that's too bad*,
which grates every time,
my husband tells me
not to be a drama queen,
that I had a jagged relationship
with my mother on a good day,
complained about her
more than he cared to listen to
and I don't know wtf to say,
have finally
passed some line,
have seen how he has
crumpled up everything
about our relationship
in one sentence,
that I crumbled
at the casual cruelty
he disguised as honesty,
have started stashing cash
as an exit strategy and
tell my sister-in-law
over lunch this week
that I have to leave
before I lose
who I am no longer sure
I am.

How to Tan With Baby Oil and Iodine

In the summer of 1981,
I found a job at Jackson Lake Park
in Lithopolis, Ohio,
as a lifeguard,
drove the 20 minutes there
(in a car I would later guilt my parents
into giving to me),
barefoot,
body sinking into the turns,
feet braced,
reckless with everything,
especially the boy who worked there,
aviator sunglasses with reflective lenses,
eyes so blue against his tan.
One look and I lost my heart.
Fraternization was not a word I knew,
nor would I have cared as I
exploded myself into his life,
his old farmhouse without a phone,
and his bed.

Reckless, too, with my parents
after having found my voice
but not having learned
to use it kindly—
I fought them on everything.

The night I snuck out the back door,
I ran barefoot to the top of the hill
and the church parking lot where
the boy waited.
Halfway to his house,
I got a bad feeling,
one I have never been able to explain,
made him take me home.

Tiptoeing across the dark living room,
my dad's voice stopped me,
but instead of anger,
I heard crying because
he thought I had run away
after a fight I had already forgotten.
The shame grew huge in my body,
still occupies a place there,
his last words stinging like a slap:
Your mother never has to know.

I Know Nothing About Chickens

Or roosters,
although once I said it sounded like
there was more than one
at the neighbor's at the lodge
where I clean most Sundays
with my friend
who said
that more than one rooster
would result in dead roosters
until there was only one standing
and I thought, *damn men.*
I wonder what it would be like
to live with only women,
think about my new guilty pleasure,
a show about plural marriage
where four women,
all married to the same man,
raise 13 children
together,
in separate houses
but sharing a backyard,
working together
and sharing a man
and I think
the man is secondary,
the real work is being a team
and supporting the others
to raise decent humans
in a world
gone crazy,
hateful speech from our leaders
balanced against
family dinners
and prayer before bed
and peaceful nights

alone in a bed
meant for two,
or more likely,
filled with children
after nightmares
or being thirsty,
children draped over each other
and spilling out of the covers,
looking like chaos,
but breathing harmony
and sleeping through the night
wrapped in arms and legs
that might not be a man's.

Finding Peace

Here,
in the cathedral
of scars,
we find some measure
of ease,
never compare,
simply listen,
perhaps
weep in solidarity,
here,
where shadows
make shapes
on pillars and
balconies
as the hours crawl
toward that crack of light
on the horizon
that signals
the start
of another day.
Of struggle?
Perhaps,
but with moments
of joy,
we pray,
knowing
it might come
with only
the promise
of more damage,
the healing
a constant for now.

Storytelling

Let me tell you a story
about a woman
and a house,
a house she loved,
a house that she poured
time and energy,
tears and swears into,
a house she knew
almost better than she knew herself,
the structure sound
until one day it was not.
Where the rot started
she didn't know,
couldn't find,
even after hours of searching.
What seemed like a small spot
growing until
the whole place
surely must collapse
and all of this happened over years,
so slowly,
and in secret places,
places she only found
by crawling deep into the house,
the basement
and the foundation,
places so broken
there was no way to fix the damage,
no saving this.

Let me tell you a story
of a woman and a house
that was never a story about houses.

This Is the Truth

When I got out of the warm bed
at 5:30 this morning
because the dog barked,
as she does earlier and earlier
despite black-out curtains
and a reflective tint on the windows near her bed
I was pissed
at you
because you are oblivious to stealth
like mine
when I have to pee during that crucial window
when the dog might wake because she hears footsteps or
the toilet lid
which I ease down
inch
by
inch
and for you not sliding
slowly
back into bed because
that damned squeaky headboard
that for almost a year didn't at all
but started again months ago
whatever magic arrangement of mattress or box springs gone
and you roll over and squeak-squeal
and you start to snore and I hear panting
and nails clicking on tile
and I pray *pleasepleasepleaseplease just another half an hour*
although I really mean two hours
but I would take fifteen minutes
or even five
and you
who woke the dog
are probably dreaming by now
and I am fumbling around

trying to find whatever warmer clothes I tossed on the floor
this week
because it is cold again this early
and I start the day angry
although if anyone asks I say *what, me angry?*
because it just isn't worth the fallout.

My mother warned me about days like this
and I can hear her voice:
you made this bed, now sleep in it.

About the Author

Kristine Williams makes her home in the hills of Athens, Ohio, where she writes about the rhythms of family and the natural world. Her poems have found their way into *The Huffington Post, Hawk and Whippoorwill, Riverwind, Women Speak, Essentially Athens Ohio, I Thought I Heard a Cardinal Sing,* and *Native Fruit.* She is the author of *Like an Empty House* (Finishing Line Press, 2020), a chapbook steeped in the quiet weight of memory. After years of teaching communication at Hocking College and Ohio University, she now tends to her writing, her garden, and the company of her husband, while her grown children carry forward her love of words and learning.

Sheila-Na-Gig Editions